It's no coincidence that when we are exposed to new experiences or times of heightened emotion we can feel more alive and inspired to change our lives. Captured fresh, these thoughts and ideas retain an honesty which, while memories mellow, will continue to comfort, challenge and inspire for years to come.

Seranders Journals will help you to record life's seminal moments in a coherent, structured way and you don't have to be a bestselling author to do it. Seranders Journals give you a basic structure to follow and there's even the Seranders' Guide to Journal Writing to give you that extra bit of inspiration.

This is a SERANDERS™ Journal

First Edition published by
SERANDERS™ in 2006.

Website
www.seranders.co.uk

E-mail
sales@seranders.co.uk
info@seranders.co.uk

Copyright © SERANDERS™ 2006

Authors: Marie & Michelle Porter

All rights reserved. No part of this publication may be reproduced, stored in a retrieval system, or transmitted in any form or by any means, electronic, mechanical, photocopying, recording, or otherwise, without the prior written permission of the copyright holder and publisher of this book.

Printed in China

ISBN 10 0-9553953-0-5
ISBN 13 978-0-9553953-0-7

IT'S ALL ABOUT
—◆—
MY TRAVELS

SERANDERS' GUIDE TO JOURNAL WRITING

One of the great things about writing is that it helps to focus your thoughts. Once penned to paper your mind is free to move on to new thought pastures - saving you from dwelling on any one aspect for too long. But how do you put the theory into practice?

This guide focuses on three key areas, 'Content', 'Structure', and 'Vocabulary'. Its usefulness will vary depending on how confident and developed your current writing style. There's no right, or wrong, way to write a journal, so these hints and tips are simply intended as a quick reference to help spark ideas and keep the ink flowing.

Content
Good journal writing is a balance of observation and self-reflection and what goes into your journal should reflect you and your experiences. Time to get the ballpoint rolling.

If you haven't written for a while it can take a little time to warm up. But as with any skill, it gets easier with practice. The trick is to start simply and use language with which you are comfortable – after all, good writing is less about long words and more about the right ones.

Still having problems putting pen to paper? Then it could simply be that you're too under-whelmed to write about anything. Thoughts or ideas don't happen in a vacuum. Think about how you're feeling, what you're thinking and the senses you're experiencing. Look for differences and similarities in the people and places you visit and start by answering some basic stimuli questions, such as what, why, when, where, how and who.

Listed below are some helpful tips and stimuli, but remember, journal writing is as much about personality as content, so go with the flow, be yourself and (most importantly) enjoy it!

- Write to an audience (even if that audience is you).

- Focus on capturing particular moments, thoughts or feelings.

- Paint pictures by drawing comparisons between your subject and recognised experiences, e.g. The man next to me smelt like old boots.

- Look for the lighter side of a situation to help inject a little humour.

- Take a break from words with cartoons or drawings.

- Capture moments while they're fresh in your mind.

- Pause to soak up your environment.

- See things from someone else's point of view - this can help spark one of your own.

- Try opening with a few different sentence styles – each can lead you in a different direction.

People: Who are they, what do they look like, where have they come from, where are they going, how do you know them, what attracted you to write about them, what are they doing, how do you interact with them, what do you share, what is different, how will you remember them.

Surroundings: Where are you, time of day, describe what it looks like, describe the flavour of the place, explain how you feel being there, think physically (geography, place, time, season, weather, landscape), think culturally (people, buildings, art, festivities, interactions, sounds, sights, smells), think personally (feelings, hopes, dreams, desires, disappointments, surprise, amazement, newness, boredom, likes, dislikes, comfort, anxiety).

Structure

Journal writing is often exploratory and it's not uncommon to not know what you want to say until you're saying it. Despite this, it helps to have a rough idea of where to start and where to end. This helps run a thread through your writing and keeps rambling tangents to a minimum.

The writer's sandwich

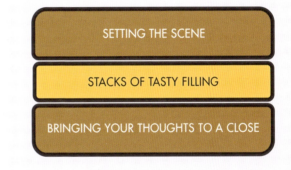

Vocabulary

People: Steely, Willowy, Sallow, Broad, Noble, Ridiculous, Enigmatic, Approachable, Fearsome, Intimidating, Gentle, Proud, Cuddly, Bearded, Sullen, Moody, Stylish, Chic, Trendy, Cool, Shallow, Elegant, Sassy, Cheeky, Arrogant.

Landscapes: Rolling, Cavernous, Verdant, Barren, Fertile, Arid, Leafy, Challenging, Hard, Gentle, Unending, Marshy, Icy, Urban, Hostile, Serene, Beautiful, Unbelievable.

Feelings: Jubilant, Distraught, Compassionate, Motivated, Apathetic, Searching, Isolated, Sensuous, Awestruck, Comfortable, Excited, Fantastic, Uneasy, Chilled, Strange.

INTRODUCTION

Whether coral gazing on the Great Barrier Reef, soul searching in the ashrams of the Indian subcontinent, or simply lapping up rays on the Med, travelling is one of life's most rewarding experiences and one, it is said, you will never forget. It's a chance to kick back, meet new people and discover new things. It may even inspire a new outlook on life. But almost as soon as you are back, you're caught up in the bustle of everyday life and the vibrancy and immediacy of your experiences fade - nearly as quickly as your tan.

This journal will help capture your trip in full Technicolor glory. The buzz, the energy, sense of adventure, people and places that inspired you, thoughts and ideas; it's all there for when you need a lift from the daily grind or simply to keep the dream alive.

THIS JOURNAL BELONGS TO:

_____

DATE

_____

CONTENTS

Travellers' Health Tips		3
Travellers' Safety Tips		6
Trip 1	Date of travel	7
Trip 2	Date of travel	15
Trip 3	Date of travel	23
Trip 4	Date of travel	31
Trip 5	Date of travel	39
Trip 6	Date of travel	47
Trip 7	Date of travel	55
Trip 8	Date of travel	63
Trip 9	Date of travel	71
Trip 10	Date of travel	79
Trip 11	Date of travel	87
Trip 12	Date of travel	95
Trip 13	Date of travel	103
Trip 14	Date of travel	111
Trip 15	Date of travel	119
Personal Information		127
Thermometer		128
Personal Notes		129

TRAVELLERS' HEALTH TIPS

How can I protect my health when I travel?

- Check the vaccinations you need to visit a country well in advance of your travel dates (just in case you have an allergic reaction). If taking oral medication, check how long before and after you have visited the country that you need to continue to take medication.

- Remember to put your insurance documents in a safe place.

- Always have your doctor's name and address noted before travelling and also the name and contact number of someone to contact in an emergency.

- Be careful of what you eat and drink.

- Always make a note of your blood type.

- List all immunisations that you have along with the expiry dates.

- Consider visiting your dentist before travelling for a check up.

- Make a note of your food and drug allergies. Note their names in the language used in the countries you are visiting.

- If you are taking medication, note their generic names as brand names can vary in other countries.

- Carry a copy of your latest eye glass prescription.

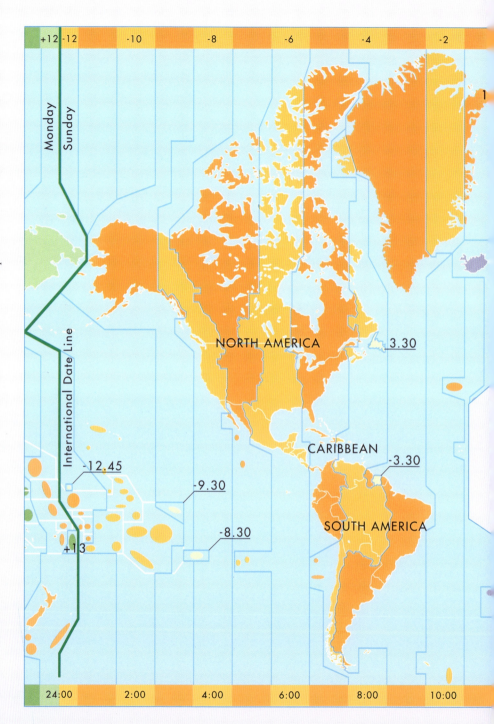

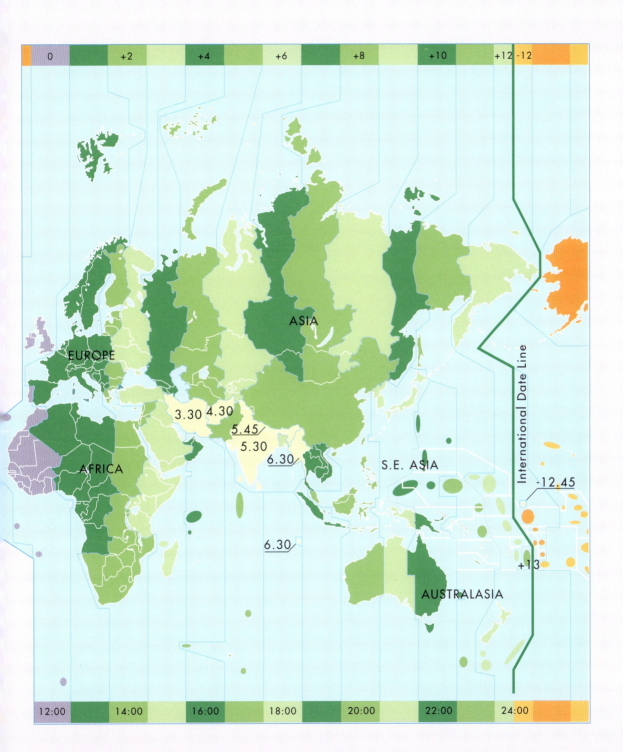

TRAVELLERS' SAFETY TIPS

How can I protect my safety while travelling?

- Before you set off, thoroughly research the destination(s) that you are travelling to so that you know of any risks associated with that country.

- Do not set out to look like a tourist. Try to blend in and dress conservatively, do not wear showy jewellery or display large amounts of cash for others to see. It's a good idea to carry just enough cash to get you through your day and leave the rest in your hotels safe.

- If you are carrying valuable items with you, ensure that you leave them in the hotels safe.

- Do not share your travel plans with strangers.

- When choosing local transportation look out for official markings. Take care when choosing taxis.

- Only board transportation from official pickup points.

- Do no accept gifts or packages from people that you do not know.

- Research the local laws and abide by them!

TRIP 1

The country/place I am visiting is

And the purpose of this trip is

Date of vacation Weather and temperature

I arrived at my destination by I stayed at

I travelled with

I met

My favourite meal was Eaten at

The places that I visited during this trip included:

If I were to go to this destination again, I would like to visit

The funniest moment was

Culturally, my impression/observations of the local people were

I purchased the following items on this trip

REFLECTIONS/MEMORIES				Date of Entry

REFLECTIONS/MEMORIES

REFLECTIONS/MEMORIES

FAVOURITE PHOTOGRAPH(S) OF VACATION

NEW FRIENDS

Name

Contact number(s)

E-mail

Address

Name

Contact number(s)

E-mail

Address

Name

Contact number(s)

E-mail

Address

Name

Contact number(s)

E-mail

Address

COLLECTABLE MEMORABILIA

(Attach items from places of interest here.)

TRIP 2

The country/place I am visiting is

And the purpose of this trip is

Date of vacation   Weather and temperature

I arrived at my destination by   I stayed at

I travelled with

I met

My favourite meal was   Eaten at

The places that I visited during this trip included:

If I were to go to this destination again, I would like to visit

The funniest moment was

Culturally, my impression/observations of the local people were

I purchased the following items on this trip

REFLECTIONS/MEMORIES   Date of Entry

REFLECTIONS/MEMORIES

REFLECTIONS/MEMORIES

FAVOURITE PHOTOGRAPH(S) OF VACATION

NEW FRIENDS

Name

Contact number(s)

E-mail

Address

Name

Contact number(s)

E-mail

Address

Name

Contact number(s)

E-mail

Address

Name

Contact number(s)

E-mail

Address

COLLECTABLE MEMORABILIA

TRIP 3

The country/place I am visiting is

And the purpose of this trip is

Date of vacation   Weather and temperature

I arrived at my destination by   I stayed at

I travelled with

I met

My favourite meal was   Eaten at

The places that I visited during this trip included:

If I were to go to this destination again, I would like to visit

The funniest moment was

Culturally, my impression/observations of the local people were

I purchased the following items on this trip

REFLECTIONS/MEMORIES   Date of Entry

REFLECTIONS/MEMORIES

REFLECTIONS/MEMORIES

FAVOURITE PHOTOGRAPH(S) OF VACATION

NEW FRIENDS

Name

Contact number(s)

E-mail

Address

Name

Contact number(s)

E-mail

Address

Name

Contact number(s)

E-mail

Address

Name

Contact number(s)

E-mail

Address

COLLECTABLE MEMORABILIA

TRIP 4

The country/place I am visiting is

And the purpose of this trip is

Date of vacation   Weather and temperature

I arrived at my destination by   I stayed at

I travelled with

I met

My favourite meal was   Eaten at

The places that I visited during this trip included:

If I were to go to this destination again, I would like to visit

The funniest moment was

Culturally, my impression/observations of the local people were

I purchased the following items on this trip

REFLECTIONS/MEMORIES

Date of Entry

REFLECTIONS/MEMORIES

REFLECTIONS/MEMORIES

FAVOURITE PHOTOGRAPH(S) OF VACATION

NEW FRIENDS

Name

Contact number(s)

E-mail

Address

Name

Contact number(s)

E-mail

Address

Name

Contact number(s)

E-mail

Address

Name

Contact number(s)

E-mail

Address

COLLECTABLE MEMORABILIA

TRIP 5

The country/place I am visiting is

And the purpose of this trip is

Date of vacation   Weather and temperature

I arrived at my destination by   I stayed at

I travelled with

I met

My favourite meal was   Eaten at

The places that I visited during this trip included:

If I were to go to this destination again, I would like to visit

The funniest moment was

Culturally, my impression/observations of the local people

were

I purchased the following items on this trip

REFLECTIONS/MEMORIES

Date of Entry

REFLECTIONS/MEMORIES

REFLECTIONS/MEMORIES

FAVOURITE PHOTOGRAPH(S) OF VACATION

NEW FRIENDS

Name

Contact number(s)

E-mail

Address

Name

Contact number(s)

E-mail

Address

Name

Contact number(s)

E-mail

Address

Name

Contact number(s)

E-mail

Address

COLLECTABLE MEMORABILIA

TRIP 6

The country/place I am visiting is

And the purpose of this trip is

Date of vacation					Weather and temperature

I arrived at my destination by			I stayed at

I travelled with

I met

My favourite meal was				Eaten at

The places that I visited during this trip included:

If I were to go to this destination again, I would like to visit

The funniest moment was

Culturally, my impression/observations of the local people were

I purchased the following items on this trip

REFLECTIONS/MEMORIES

Date of Entry

REFLECTIONS/MEMORIES

REFLECTIONS/MEMORIES

FAVOURITE PHOTOGRAPH(S) OF VACATION

NEW FRIENDS

Name

Contact number(s)

E-mail

Address

Name

Contact number(s)

E-mail

Address

Name

Contact number(s)

E-mail

Address

Name

Contact number(s)

E-mail

Address

COLLECTABLE MEMORABILIA

TRIP 7

The country/place I am visiting is

And the purpose of this trip is

Date of vacation   Weather and temperature

I arrived at my destination by   I stayed at

I travelled with

I met

My favourite meal was   Eaten at

The places that I visited during this trip included:

If I were to go to this destination again, I would like to visit

The funniest moment was

Culturally, my impression/observations of the local people were

I purchased the following items on this trip

REFLECTIONS/MEMORIES

Date of Entry

REFLECTIONS/MEMORIES

REFLECTIONS/MEMORIES

FAVOURITE PHOTOGRAPH(S) OF VACATION

NEW FRIENDS

Name

Contact number(s)

E-mail

Address

Name

Contact number(s)

E-mail

Address

Name

Contact number(s)

E-mail

Address

Name

Contact number(s)

E-mail

Address

COLLECTABLE MEMORABILIA

TRIP 8

The country/place I am visiting is

And the purpose of this trip is

Date of vacation   Weather and temperature

I arrived at my destination by   I stayed at

I travelled with

I met

My favourite meal was   Eaten at

The places that I visited during this trip included:

If I were to go to this destination again, I would like to visit

The funniest moment was

Culturally, my impression/observations of the local people were

I purchased the following items on this trip

REFLECTIONS/MEMORIES   Date of Entry

REFLECTIONS/MEMORIES

REFLECTIONS/MEMORIES

FAVOURITE PHOTOGRAPH(S) OF VACATION

NEW FRIENDS

Name

Contact number(s)

E-mail

Address

Name

Contact number(s)

E-mail

Address

Name

Contact number(s)

E-mail

Address

Name

Contact number(s)

E-mail

Address

COLLECTABLE MEMORABILIA

TRIP 9

The country/place I am visiting is

And the purpose of this trip is

Date of vacation — Weather and temperature

I arrived at my destination by — I stayed at

I travelled with

I met

My favourite meal was — Eaten at

The places that I visited during this trip included:

If I were to go to this destination again, I would like to visit

The funniest moment was

Culturally, my impression/observations of the local people were

I purchased the following items on this trip

REFLECTIONS/MEMORIES

Date of Entry

REFLECTIONS/MEMORIES

REFLECTIONS/MEMORIES

FAVOURITE PHOTOGRAPH(S) OF VACATION

NEW FRIENDS

Name

Contact number(s)

E-mail

Address

Name

Contact number(s)

E-mail

Address

Name

Contact number(s)

E-mail

Address

Name

Contact number(s)

E-mail

Address

COLLECTABLE MEMORABILIA

TRIP 10

The country/place I am visiting is

And the purpose of this trip is

Date of vacation   Weather and temperature

I arrived at my destination by   I stayed at

I travelled with

I met

My favourite meal was   Eaten at

The places that I visited during this trip included:

If I were to go to this destination again, I would like to visit

The funniest moment was

Culturally, my impression/observations of the local people were

I purchased the following items on this trip

REFLECTIONS/MEMORIES Date of Entry

REFLECTIONS/MEMORIES

REFLECTIONS/MEMORIES

FAVOURITE PHOTOGRAPH(S) OF VACATION

NEW FRIENDS

Name

Contact number(s)

E-mail

Address

Name

Contact number(s)

E-mail

Address

Name

Contact number(s)

E-mail

Address

Name

Contact number(s)

E-mail

Address

COLLECTABLE MEMORABILIA

TRIP 11

The country/place I am visiting is

And the purpose of this trip is

Date of vacation   Weather and temperature

I arrived at my destination by   I stayed at

I travelled with

I met

My favourite meal was   Eaten at

The places that I visited during this trip included:

If I were to go to this destination again, I would like to visit

The funniest moment was

Culturally, my impression/observations of the local people were

I purchased the following items on this trip

REFLECTIONS/MEMORIES

Date of Entry

REFLECTIONS/MEMORIES

REFLECTIONS/MEMORIES

FAVOURITE PHOTOGRAPH(S) OF VACATION

NEW FRIENDS

Name

Contact number(s)

E-mail

Address

Name

Contact number(s)

E-mail

Address

Name

Contact number(s)

E-mail

Address

Name

Contact number(s)

E-mail

Address

COLLECTABLE MEMORABILIA

TRIP 12

The country/place I am visiting is

And the purpose of this trip is

Date of vacation											Weather and temperature

I arrived at my destination by								I stayed at

I travelled with

I met

My favourite meal was										Eaten at

The places that I visited during this trip included:

If I were to go to this destination again, I would like to visit

The funniest moment was

Culturally, my impression/observations of the local people were

I purchased the following items on this trip

REFLECTIONS/MEMORIES   Date of Entry

REFLECTIONS/MEMORIES

REFLECTIONS/MEMORIES

FAVOURITE PHOTOGRAPH(S) OF VACATION

NEW FRIENDS

Name

Contact number(s)

E-mail

Address

Name

Contact number(s)

E-mail

Address

Name

Contact number(s)

E-mail

Address

Name

Contact number(s)

E-mail

Address

COLLECTABLE MEMORABILIA

TRIP 13

The country/place I am visiting is

And the purpose of this trip is

Date of vacation   Weather and temperature

I arrived at my destination by   I stayed at

I travelled with

I met

My favourite meal was   Eaten at

The places that I visited during this trip included:

If I were to go to this destination again, I would like to visit

The funniest moment was

Culturally, my impression/observations of the local people were

I purchased the following items on this trip

REFLECTIONS/MEMORIES

Date of Entry

REFLECTIONS/MEMORIES

REFLECTIONS/MEMORIES

FAVOURITE PHOTOGRAPH(S) OF VACATIONS

NEW FRIENDS

Name

Contact number(s)

E-mail

Address

Name

Contact number(s)

E-mail

Address

Name

Contact number(s)

E-mail

Address

Name

Contact number(s)

E-mail

Address

COLLECTABLE MEMORABILIA

TRIP 14

The country/place I am visiting is

And the purpose of this trip is

Date of vacation   Weather and temperature

I arrived at my destination by   I stayed at

I travelled with

I met

My favourite meal was   Eaten at

The places that I visited during this trip included:

If I were to go to this destination again, I would like to visit

The funniest moment was

Culturally, my impression/observations of the local people were

I purchased the following items on this trip

REFLECTIONS/MEMORIES

Date of Entry

REFLECTIONS/MEMORIES

REFLECTIONS/MEMORIES

FAVOURITE PHOTOGRAPH(S) OF VACATIONS

NEW FRIENDS

Name

Contact number(s)

E-mail

Address

Name

Contact number(s)

E-mail

Address

Name

Contact number(s)

E-mail

Address

Name

Contact number(s)

E-mail

Address

COLLECTABLE MEMORABILIA

TRIP 15

The country/place I am visiting is

And the purpose of this trip is

Date of vacation   Weather and temperature

I arrived at my destination by   I stayed at

I travelled with

I met

My favourite meal was   Eaten at

The places that I visited during this trip included:

If I were to go to this destination again, I would like to visit

The funniest moment was

Culturally, my impression/observations of the local people were

I purchased the following items on this trip

REFLECTIONS/MEMORIES

Date of Entry

REFLECTIONS/MEMORIES

REFLECTIONS/MEMORIES

FAVOURITE PHOTOGRAPH(S) OF VACATIONS

NEW FRIENDS

Name

Contact number(s)

E-mail

Address

Name

Contact number(s)

E-mail

Address

Name

Contact number(s)

E-mail

Address

Name

Contact number(s)

E-mail

Address

COLLECTABLE MEMORABILIA

PERSONAL INFORMATION

Name

Address

Telephone

Email

Bank

Bank Tel. Number

Credit Card Tel. Number

Mobile Provider Tel. Number

Blood Group

Passport Number

Expiry Date

Organ donor information

Medical Insurance Company

Address

Telephone

Policy Number

Rental Car Company

Driving Licence Number

Internet Access Provider

In case of an emergency, please notify:

Name

Telephone (day & mobile)

Doctor

Doctor's Tel. Number

Known allergies

Medication(s) taken

THERMOMETER

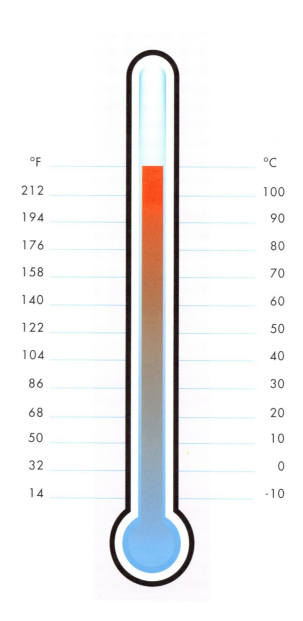

NOTES

NOTES

NOTES

Additional titles also available from SERANDERS™ include:

It's All About…

My Life

Relocating

Student Life

My Holidays
(Children's Journal)

Our Wedding

Remembrance
(Bereavement)